Living Like A Champion

Winning In Your Own Lane

David McGahey

Copyright Page:

any other jurisdiction is the sole responsibility of the reader and consumer.

Neither the author nor the publisher assumes any responsibility or liability whatsoever on behalf of the consumer or reader of this material. Any perceived slight of any individual or organisation is purely unintentional.

The resources in this book are provided for informational purposes only and should not be used to replace the specialised training and professional judgement of a health care or mental health care professional.

Neither the author nor the publisher can be held responsible for the use of the information provided within this book. Please always consult a trained professional before making any decision regarding treatment of yourself or others.

For more information, email pastor.david@nlfc.ie

Dedication

This book is dedicated to every self-doubting child of God out there, of which I am one. We spend so much of our time comparing our success to that of others, and as a result, settling for less of an existence than that we were created for.

Wherefore seeing we also are compassed about with so great a cloud of witnesses, let us lay aside every weight, and the sin which doth so easily beset us, and let us run with patience the race that is set before us, looking unto Jesus the author and finisher of our faith; who for the joy that was set before him endured the cross, despising the shame, and is set down at the right hand of the throne of God. ***Hebrews 12:1-2 KJV***

Table of Contents:

Jude 1:24-25

King James Version (KJV)

Now unto him that is able to keep you from falling, and to present you faultless before the presence of his glory with exceeding joy, to the only wise God our Saviour, be glory and majesty, dominion and power, both now and ever.

Introduction:

Although I have had most of the content for this book for many years, I have put off writing it for the same reasons you may be thinking about my book too. I am not a MEGA Success in life. I have not earned millions; I don't pastor a church of thousands. I am quite ordinary, in comparison to many industry leaders. But this book aims to demolish this exact line of thinking. I know I am not the best there is, but I now know, that I am the best I need to be in my lane. Why? Well, I am the only one there. God has not purposed you to race against others, your race, your lane, is set up specifically for you, to be run by you, to be won by you.

But many of us are bowing out of the personal race of purpose because we are fixed on the lives of other people. There is a champion inside each one of us, set up for success, set out to win, but like the natural champions around us, it calls for discipline in our living, and in our thinking to get us there.

I've lived a life always feeling like the most underqualified person in the room, never wanting to engage with peers. But over the past few years, I have become comfortable with the knowledge that I am running my own race, at God's set pace, and I am not in last place. I want to share with you some of the principles that have accompanied my life and journey, and that has brought me to a place where I know I am on course to finish strong, that which God has laid out before me.
So why a book now? Well, I strongly believe we are to redeem our time in this ever-growing world of evil. And I am also confident that what God has revealed to me, developed in me, and coached me through can be a blessing to you, on your journey.

And as you read this my prayer truly is, that you will be armed with tools that will allow you to be the Champion of your own lane. That you too will understand that you are running your own race, at God's set pace, and you are not in last place!

Chapter 1

Champions Follow The Coaches Plan

1 Corinthians 9 24-27 KJV Know ye not that they which run in a race run all, but one recieveth the prize? So run, that ye may obtain. And every man that striveth for the mastery is temperate in all things. Now they do it to obtain a corruptible crown; but we incorruptible. I therefore so run, not as uncertainly; so fight I , not as one that beateth the air. But I keep under my body, and bring it into subjection: lest that by any means, when I have preached to others, I myself should be a castaway.

Throughout this chapter and in some others to follow you will see me often give reference to athletes and their respective fields of sport. The truth is I have never had much interest in sports growing up, aside from track and field, I have never really had any passion for them.

But even with that said I have always had an admiration and great respect for the dedication of these professionals to their relevant disciplines. I've identified from an early age that there is an earthly commitment from champions to winning that is rarely mirrored in any other space of life. Most of us want to join a field and be part of the mix, but every world-stage athlete strives to be the greatest of all time. Participating is not enough for them. They display a dedication to winning for the glory, the title, and the gold medal. To receive a trophy that fades and tarnishes, to become part of a celebration that erases with time. I mean can you tell me who won the world cup in 1962 without using Google? Doubtful!

The truth is we remember very few of the champions of times past. Nevertheless, athletes will devote their entire living, diet, and habits to one race, one fight, for a moment in the spotlight and a passing sense of achievement.

As a spectator, it can be baffling when we see how some fights, especially in sports like MMA last only seconds, yet the commitment towards the goal is pursued over months if not years. I don't believe there is any athlete in the world that would be happy to be identified as an overnight success. We simply see in a flash what was cultivated over a long time, with great sacrifice and extreme focus. And all this is done just for the natural sense of victory that will fade over the years.

So needless to say as Christians it's shocking how we seem to want to operate our spiritual lives in complete opposition to this natural display of discipline. We often expect a lifelong victory to be gained from a two-minute commitment to our faith. As though we have never read the scriptures and have mistaken God's word as a quick fix to success. Honestly, in this Christian life, it appears as though we want to get as much as possible from as little effort as needed, everyone battling for viral fame and instant recognition. But the reality is, and what I have experienced, is that the effort put in is usually always way more, far longer, and often harder than the victory experienced.

The root has to grow much deeper than we realize, to produce the fruit we want to actualize. It requires cultivating the soil of our lives, digging and unearthing bad seed that has formed choking weeds to our destiny, replanting and watering, patiently waiting and trusting that one day the fruit that appears before men will be of the good that we have invested. Our years in the limelight of purpose will only last a fraction of the years that were invested in our development.

Paul in the scripture above is telling us that we are competing for a greater purpose, one that isn't fleeting and will not tarnish, an eternal gold, an eternal reward. He lets us know this prize is worth all of his life and energy, all of his discipline, and focus. Yet often we tend to not display even a fraction of the behaviors and habits of ordinary champions, in our lives of faith and our pursuit of purpose.

I truly believe if you would emulate the habits outlined in this book if you could model these behaviours, then you would experience a different level of victory in your lane, and you would create a different level of glory for your future. Producing a far greater level of glory for God through your life, your church, your city, and your nation.

What's important to note right off the bat is that every successful athlete follows a successful plan. And that athlete is committed not to his own plan, but to the one set out by his seasoned coach. Every great athlete has obtained an even greater coach who has mapped out his strategy for winning. Why? Why does the young ambitious athlete trust the strategy of the coach, often forcing him to surrender to his own pride and tactics? Because he understands something, the coach has years of expertise and experience on the athlete, the coach is no longer in the game but he has the winning strategy.

Even in my own life, there were so many times I wished I had listened to the instruction and advice of those around me who tried to coach me, who had lived longer than me, parents, youth leaders, and pastors who from their encounters and experiences tried to save me from many mistakes along the way. Let me if I may in this chapter, challenge the attitude within all of us that tells us- this is my life to live, it's me facing the battles daily, I am the one braving the storms, not God, so "I'll go my way".
But here's the truth, God has been there, God has weathered more than you or I ever will. He has seen more victory than you or I will ever get to glimpse. So we can choose to battle through life's situations and circumstances and do it our way, with little to no impact most of the time, or, we can seek out His strategy in all of life's issues. His instruction will always lead you to His results after all.

So for the purpose of this exercise let's refer to God as our Coach with a capital 'C'.

A coach of any natural athlete will set out a plan for the success of said athlete, from sleep habits to diet, to the right fitness regime. And an athlete may pass McDonald's, saliva dripping from his mouth at the thoughts of a big mac with chips, but ultimately, because of what he wants to achieve, he won't stray from his commitment to the plan he has been set. That is if he is really serious about being a champion in his field then he will avoid giving in to that which holds him back.

Now you and me- we may go to the gym, we may go for a run, maybe even lift an odd kettlebell here and there. But we will still get the big mac and chips if we truly want to, why? Well, because we aren't that serious about our physical condition or the sport, we aren't committed to victory, and we certainly have not surrendered ourselves to a coach's plan. And that's fine, honestly, very few of us reading this book are trying to be the next Lionel Messi in the world of football.

But when it comes to our spiritual living we cannot afford to be so flippant with the plans of our Coach. I along with many others in the kingdom have such a sense of urgency regarding time, and it is time for the church of God to become deadly serious about running our race to win! It is not enough anymore to just get through it, we need to find the zeal that Paul describes to win in our lane.

No More Sloppy Living.

Maybe you are already considering while reading this, how much or how little dedication you may have to your lane. Well let me help by pointing out that the evidence for that is not in how much you have achieved but it is truly in the degree of commitment you hold to the strategy of God in your life.

Proverbs 16:3 KJV Commit your works unto the Lord and thy thoughts shall be established.

We are instructed by the Coach to commit our works to Him. To commit something to someone means to put them in charge of it, or, to trust them with it. So by very definition, God should be in charge of your ways. We are not our own CEO, that position has to be handed over to God, we start winning by surrendering our plans for His.

And may I just be real with you for a moment - His strategy never really made sense to me in the early days, there was more discipline than elevation, and more steadfastness required of me than displays of great progress. I knew God had a calling on my life from a young age, but God's path for me to be where I am today was filled with serving in areas that had nothing to do with my ambitions. Constantly being overlooked for tasks I felt ready for, and chosen for things at times I honestly felt were beneath me. I spent years in obscurity amongst the church long after I had been to bible school, years before God ever asked me to preach a single message. But one thing has always been consistent about me, I was and am surrendered to the Coach, if He asked it I did it. If he opened an area of opportunity I walked into it, it didn't always look like how I would have planned it, but it always produced in me what was needed in those moments of my life, preparing me for each next stage.

I always think about the scene in the movie Karate Kid, where Mr.Miyagi begins training Daniel by having him clean his car, "wax on, wax off", which echoes through my brain every time I recollect the scene. And the perplexed student, not understanding how cleaning this car is bringing him closer to being a champion of karate. How he becomes frequently frustrated at his lack of obvious progress. In fact, it isn't until much later in the movie that the purpose of the discipline is revealed to the student.

Today if we want to be a champion we need to decide to say a complete yes to the coach's plan, we cannot sway somewhere in the middle. And His training and molding of us may not look as we expected it, like Daniel waxing a car instead of learning martial arts, but we need to trust enough that whatever the Master says- we do, no questions asked. Trusting that His purpose will be revealed through the process.

Truthfully, we could give Coach our yes and He may place us in an area of service that we see as having nothing to do with our purpose, but understand there is value in His method of training. It may feel like cleaning cars when you want to be on the mat. But what He is building in you right now through His tailored training program is vital to your success when He places you firmly in your lane.

We see that scripture calls us to give God our ways, but, what are your ways? Well simply said your ways are your habits, your spiritual diet, your vocation, and your calling. These are key areas of our lives that should be led by God, and implemented by us just as the Coach desires. If we are to live the life of a champion then we need to follow the plan of our coach in all of these areas.

Matthew 6:33 King James Version (KJV) 33 But seek ye first the kingdom of God, and his righteousness; and all these things shall be added unto you.

God's strategy, His plan to which you should be committed to- is to seek His kingdom first in our lives. Place what concerns the Kingdom as the highest priority in your habits and your living. Now to seek first means it's ok to seek secondly after some other stuff, sure it's ok to seek after a job, the bible teaches that we should work and not be lazy - but if you seek His kingdom first then the right job will be added to you. Seek the job first and you may not be in the place God has called you to. And a good measure of whether God has added your job to your life is to ask - if your job is preventing you from serving, pursuing, and growing in God if so then it's not the job He has designed for you.

And if you are going to run to win, if you want to be a champion in the race of life, you have got to take the Coach's plan in every area, every time. It's ok to want nice things, to want a nice car, a nice home, but seek the kingdom first and nice things will be added to you out of God's supply. If you seek the things first you'll likely seek the provision from outside of God's hand and as a result, always have less than what God could provide.

If I want to be a champion in life as a believer, it starts as simply as deciding to be committed to God's plan, committed to seeking the Kingdom first with all of my energy.

Daniel in the Old Testament is a model example of someone who committed their ways to the Coach and saw the elevation in life that this brings about. And I can hear you say- hold on, isn't there a better example of a champion to follow in scripture, after all, Daniel is the one who got thrown into Lion's den. And to that, I say, how else can we test our commitment without putting it against a trial? Sometimes our Coach will allow a trial and test to come our way. Not to defeat you, not to knock you out of the race, but to see if push comes to shove you are committed to this thing or not.

Jumping back to the Karate Kid and the final fight, we see young Daniel cheated by the opponent, we find him injured, his circumstance is so unfair at this moment, and we the audience are gutted for him. We must note though that Daniel's coach didn't provide the enemy, he didn't tell the enemy to play dirty, and the enemy had his own coach that he was listening to. Daniel's coach however also didn't step in and save him when he got knocked down, he didn't call him out of the ring, he stood and watched, his disposition didn't change because he knew that if Daniel would just stay in the fight, just stay committed in the battle, that he had what it took within him, for him to win. After all, he had committed his ways to his coach, he made a pact to do what he was told without question. And under the test what was put in him came out as a chilling victory! You can't watch this scene without wanting to leap up and cheer for him.

But earlier in the movie the coach wasn't willing to stay out of it, there is a scene in the movie where Daniel is ambushed by a bunch of kids from the neighboring dojo, and none of his training was yet developed in him, which led to him getting his butt kicked. Then out of the mist Mr.Miyagi steps in and defends his student warding off the enemies. This could have been an opportunity for Daniel to question the training process. But the reality is Daniel found himself in a battle he wasn't prepared for, and like a great coach, he stepped in to defend him.

It's a great comfort to know that God will always defend us when we jump out ahead of the plan. But there are times when the development dismisses the need for the defense of God. He knows what is in you is enough. His silence in the battle is an affirmation that you're ready, not a sign of your abandonment.

Now let's look at the other Daniel again here in the scriptures- let me provide a little background on this kid, he was chosen by Nebuchadnezzar to stand in the palace courts because of his wisdom, we know one of the greatest qualities of Daniel's life was his devotion to the instruction of his Coach. One of the kings' stipulations for the role Daniel stepped into, was for the chosen kids to eat the royal diet. This went against the diet set out for Daniel from God's word and he didn't want to defile himself by eating this diet or drinking the wine so he chose to challenge it. He said he would only continue to eat vegetables and they could assess whether he was any worse off for the diet than the other kids after ten days. They agreed and low and behold Daniel it says in scripture was more robust than the others, so they allowed him to remain on this diet.

Again straight off we see-

His commitment to the Coach was more important than the opportunities in life.

In fact, Daniel would happily challenge the opportunity to allow him to carry out His commitment to God and knew if the opportunity fell through it was never from God anyway. Some of us need to start being brave enough to challenge life's opportunities with the commitments we have made to God. If it's agreeable to the plan of the Coach then embrace it, if it's not then drop it, and understand it never came from God, so it will never truly add to or fulfill your life.

Please remember, your God won't provide something for you that will move you far from Him, but guess what, the devil will. He will happily give you a great job, in a great location, with tons of great opportunities, that will pay great! As long as it pushes a wedge between you and your pursuit of Christ. Personally, I have never accepted a job that did not contractually accept the fact that I was a churchgoer and that I would not work on Sunday mornings. This was a value I refused to compromise on.

I decided if my life was committed to God then the right job would be proposed by Him and therefore not interfere with His purposes. And every job attached to my purpose has embraced this, and any job that was even hesitant or vague around this allowance, I rejected, without another thought. This allowed me to flourish in both my understanding of God through the teaching of pastors I sat under week in and week out, and also caused me to flourish in my service of God as I was able to be fully committed to whatever ministry I volunteered for.

So here is Daniel, a vegetarian, refusing to partake in the standard diet, fully committed to God, and still being elevated to success naturally in the palace. Daniel remains there for some time until in chapter six, where we find Nebuchadnezzar replaced by Darius as king. At this time Daniel is so elevated above the others that Darius puts him in charge of the kingdom. Come on, how much more encouragement do you and I need, if you commit your ways to God He will elevate you in life above others, you will stand out, you will be promotable, and you will get opportunities you aren't even qualified for because you're seeking first the kingdom of God.

And like every new king Darius is changing things up in the Kingdom. And he's not interested in the peoples' diet like his predecessor, no he's much more afflicted with the people's devotion to him as their ruler. So the other palace courts men, who were so envious of Daniel and so aware of Daniel's devotion to God, seeing the king's insecurity, pushed for a decree that no one could pray to any god for 30 days, and prayers could only be offered to Darius the King.

The king backed this happily as it gloried himself above even the gods. And of course, it wasn't long until Daniel was found praying to the true God. (Daniel 6:10) When Daniel learned that the decree had been signed and posted, he continued to pray just as he had always done. His house had windows in the upstairs that opened toward Jerusalem. Three times a day he knelt there in prayer, thanking and praising his God.

Commitment means that even when the world is going another way, I'm going to stick with the plan of my Coach.

And we know how the story of Daniel plays out. He is reported for praying and is tossed into the den of Lions. This is the point in our lives where we expect the Coach to tap us out. For God to remove us from the approaching danger. But He doesn't.
Daniel faces what man had set up to destroy him, but in true fashion, God uses it for His glory. Daniel stuck to the plan of the Coach even when it looked naturally like it was leading to his detriment.

Don't disappoint those who think they are setting you up for destruction by caving in or running off, face off the challenge and let them see that Your God to whom you are loyal is going to bring you victory!

Both Daniels we spoke of in this chapter experienced what it meant to be a champion, to have victory, to see great challenges and remain on course, to have unfair circumstances thrown at them and yet stick to the strategy of the Coach. To be the underdog but to be led to the greatest victory. In the scriptures Daniel's Commitment elevated him at a young age, he was challenged by his enemies, and punishment was enforced by his superior, but because of commitment, God championed him. He came out of death's face without a tooth mark on his skin, and in his victory, God received much glory!

Never downplay your obedience.

The whole kingdom was instructed to worship the God of Daniel, because of what was produced in Daniel's commitment to God, a kingdom was led to acknowledge Him as the one true God.

And that is the true mark of a champion in God, someone who doesn't just elevate their own living but imparts something to their generation, that elevates the living of a whole society in line with the Kingdom. We all have this potential. We all have this opportunity. Not all will rise to it though because not all of us are willing to be that committed to the plans of the Coach for us.

But maybe today you are. Maybe today you are beginning to read this book and thinking that I want that to be me. Can I start this journey by telling you that the first rule in living as a champion is **committing your ways to God, seeking His kingdom, following His plan and His regime**, is **being brave enough to challenge opportunity with your commitments** and keep the Coaches plan central, even when the world is moving in a different direction. Then you will overcome every trial, have victory in all situations, and in all of your victories God will be honored. As you are being elevated He is being glorified.

Let us pray together- Dear Lord, I need your help through your Holy Spirit, to guide me in your ways, to address areas within me that remain unsurrendered to your plan. Help me be brave enough to always seek Kingdom things first, trusting that you are caring for my needs and wants. Spirit of God begin a work within me, shaping me to be the champion I am called to be, in the lane I have been purposed to run in. Amen.

NOTES

Chapter 2

Champions Deal With The Pains Of Growing

James 1:2-4 KJV My brethren, count it all joy when ye fall into divers temptations; knowing this, that the trying of your faith worketh patience. But let patience have her perfect work, that ye may be perfect and entire, wanting nothing.

One standout attitude of a Champion is that they choose to deal with the pains of growing. James paints a very unattractive picture here of spiritual growth, growing through trials and tests. Letting pressure encourage endurance and endurance produce the perfect result.

Wouldn't it truly be so much better, if we could be perfected in any other way? But sadly, even the idea of pressure causes some of us to live in unfinished states, settling in places of comfort instead of growing through places of testing.

So much of what we value naturally was produced under extreme conditions- Diamonds, Rubies, Emeralds, and Sapphires are all produced under immense pressure far beneath the surface of the earth. We look at the finished beauty and value the end result so greatly, we pay huge prices to wear these things on our ears or around our fingers. We hold them so precious they become symbols of our eternal love for the one we would marry.

But the greatest beauty in all of these things is often missed, the real value came through their development under harsh testing.

We all want to be the diamond- valued and seen as something of beauty to others, but not all of us are willing to endure what the diamond did to get there, after all a diamond was once only a rock.

Ever worked out at the gym? I have, and I hate it. I have at some stage across the years been a member of every gym my town has to offer, paid crazy money in minding fees (minding the building in case one day I decide to physically go). The truth is I actually love the idea of working out and looking good, getting beach ready every summer but staying winter insulated all year round instead. And do you know why I fail to transform my body every single time? Why I can balance my coffee cup on my stomach while I write this sentence?

Well you know the point where your muscles are in agony from the bicep curls and you feel like you have no more reps in you? That squat that was just a little bit harder than you wanted it to be? The push-up that makes you want to give up? Well apparently it's only what you do onwards from that point that builds on the muscles you already have? And this is the point I stop pushing, call it a day, and head to the sauna, so no wonder why I never grow on the basic muscles I have developed, I am not willing to work past my place of comfort. I won't let endurance have its perfect work. And it's not just physical growth that is uncomfortable.

Spiritual growth has pains that come with it too!

Pains from being stretched, aches from being challenged, tiredness from carrying a new weight of responsibility. And yet we are called to realize that it is only what we do once we have reached the end of what is comfortable that adds to our strength and pushes us towards greater victory in Christ. We too often look at our current discomfort as a sign to abandon the thing we have set our hand or heart to, but it is the barometer of our comfort not the alarm for our abandonment.

If we would learn to push through the pain we would live to see greater transformation in our way of thinking and operating, and we would experience levels of victory far beyond what we currently see as possible.

One of my all-time favorite movies is called- Facing The Giants, this is not a movie with a huge budget or star-studded cast, but the revelations from this movie have done more for my life than I have time to document in this book. In the movie we are introduced to a losing high school football team, who coast through each practice session, complaining of how they never win, with a coach failing in every corner of life - from work achievements to home management.

But then we get to see into one particular practice session where the coach, after going through personal work with God, notices the negative influence one of the players is having on the whole team during their practices. So he pulls the kid out from the crowd and asks him to do the death crawl exercise (to get down on all fours and crawl up the field with another kid on his back), but he instructs the kid that he must give his absolute best. After some back and forth between them the kid agrees to give it all he has. The coach then adds a blindfold to the equation, so that the kids' mindset won't cause him to give up once he is happy with how far he has gone when he truly held the potential to go further.

So off he goes crawling up the field, with another kid latched to his back. The kid starts strong, but soon he is found battling it out, telling the coach it hurts, and asking the coach how far he has gone, the coach doesn't tell him to stop at this point, he doesn't let him know how far he has traveled, but instead roars at him to keep going to give his very best, don't quit, keep going he repeats over and over. The pain is obvious on the face of the kid, he is no longer comfortable, sweat is beading down his face, and he hasn't endured this length of the task before. But the cheering and encouragement of the coach causes him to push through, to keep crawling even while in pain and while wanting to quit, choosing instead to endure the task. In the end, the kid who at the start simply wanted to make it twenty yards crossed the one-hundred-yard line, showing himself and the others on his team that there is definitely more to give but it's certainly gonna hurt.

It's such an emotional scene for me, I struggle to hold back tears each time I watch it, even after all of these years. Because every time I watch it I cannot help but recount the times I felt like it was too hard to keep going. The many, many occasions that I wanted to quit and just settle where I was at.

But I could see how in each of these times the action of God in my own life reflected the actions of the coach in the movie, always cheering me on, yelling at me to give it my best, telling me to not quit, to keep going. Always knowing that there was more in me to be discovered, reminding me that I am far from fully developed. Learning to trust this voice intimately through difficult seasons, well after all He did form me and craft me for the very things He was leading me into didn't He?

The simple truth is that there have been times I have felt like it hurt too much to continue but by the grace of my God, through the encouragement of His Spirit, and by pressing forward I have grown in greater ways through testing environments than any comfortable season has ever caused me to.

The fact is that we all know where and how far we can go with life in order to stay in our comfort zone. We have all taped out the boundaries of comfort around us, and many of us live year in and year out being successful within our circle of comfort. But without ever truly growing.

When is the last time we allowed testing, pain, and trial to sculpt us, stretch us, and grow us? When will we become dissatisfied enough with where we are at in our spiritual journey to finally put up with the growing pains? Lord shake up our apathy toward our destiny.

A true trick of the most successful athletes in the world is that champions don't just deal with the pains of growing, they use them as motivation. Knowing they are building strength and conditioning themselves for further success causes them to push through the agony of development. Take note of that, how the pains of your current season should fuel you to build on your strengths and push you further into success. After all the pains are only there to benchmark your comfort and highlight that you are entering into a zone of growth. But if you're like me at the gym the moment those signs of growth appear in the form of discomfort you want to stop pushing. And then we sit back in amazement wondering why we can't get ripped.

We all want God to guide us to greatness, but few understand that when God brings us from one level to the next in life it often involves a challenging transition. And what we don't tend to settle in ourselves is that how we are in the transition is usually determinative of where we get to in the next stage we are entering.

Or.....how I handle the pains of growth determines how tall or how strong I can become in my destiny.

We must understand that God won't force change on you but He can't elevate you in this life without first shaping you. There is a frequently used yet underestimated statement in life that simply says "No Pain – No Gain" And any of you who have lived long enough on this earth know this to be oh-so-true. Now I don’t mean pain as in sorrow or despair but rather the nagging pains and discomforts of growth, the stretch in new situations that pushes us to apply ourselves more and trust God deeper.

The twinge in our muscles that say you can’t handle this pressure and responsibility- give up. And I think it is vital for us to identify between the two- from times when we are truly hurting and need the nurturing care of our God, to times we are simply being stretched.

My son often comes to me with pains in his legs- when these first began to appear he always thought he was hurt or injured in some way, but now through identifying this source of pain and seeing its work carried out, he assures me "these are probably growing pains, Dad". As a good dad, I would never ignore or cause my son to walk on injured legs, but I also know enough to not interfere, or allow his life to be held back by the niggling pains of growth. This is a good healthy sign that my boy is growing. So I don't insist on him leaping onto the couch and resting, I simply affirm to him that yes son these are growing pains, you will be fine, on you go and get on with the day.

Don't delay your destiny any longer by resting because of pains that are there to simply show that you are growing.

Let me show you in scripture a great journey of championship stature that went sour because the people could not embrace the pains of growth. In Exodus, we see the Israelites receive many miracles performed by God in Egypt and later in the desert. Firstly, there were the ten plagues in Egypt that led to their freedom (Exodus 7:17 to 12:33) then the parting of the Red Sea that swallowed their enemy (Exodus 14:16 to 22). Then as they traveled through the desert they had an incredible, supernatural cloud by day to lead and protect them, and a fire by night to lead and warm them (Exodus 13:21). Nothing was burned by this pillar of fire – it was wholly supernatural – yet the Israelites became fearful and complained against God for it. The Lord purified bitter water to quench their thirst (Exodus 15:23 to 25). God gave them Manna to eat to dull their pangs of hunger (Exodus 16:14 & 15) which was angel's food (Psalm 78:25) but they complained about it (Numbers 11:1 to 13). God gave them quail to eat (Exodus 16:13). They saw God bring water out of a rock (Exodus 17:6). That Rock supernaturally followed them as they journeyed and yet they moaned against Moses (Exodus 14:11 & 12). At one point they wanted to stone Moses (Exodus 17:2 to

4). God gave them everything they wanted and needed to prove that He was taking care of them and they still complained about their hardships (Numbers 11:1).

You see to understand their lament we must remember that the children of Israel were in slavery to the Egyptians for over four hundred years according to scripture. So, several generations grew up living as second-class citizens, slaves, and people accustomed to defeat. And not only this but they became good at it, they were known to the Egyptians as hard workers.

The Israelites were always looking towards freedom, but truth be told they were not ready for the internal growth that would have to take place to step into the new season of dependency on their Lord. God in His awesome power and mercy freed the Israelites through Moses, and in the challenging transition, they were forced to be confronted with some natural growing pains. You see they are discovering that they hadn't just had a slave experience they had been conditioned with a slave mentality. They were now having to learn to trust God through faith for His provision and to be grateful for what He would provide. Up to now, they had been used to taking what the Egyptians had to give them, now they had to shift their dependency and trust to God.

They were constantly griping over what God provided, they wanted provision to look the way they were used to it being. They are noted as having stated that they would have been better off left as slaves in Egypt because at least then they would have been fed right. Now remember God's ultimate goal here is to provide for the people a promised land, a place to inherit. They knew this, God had communicated it. They understood what they were working towards, but they couldn't even find gratitude for the food being sent from heaven in the face of their harsh testing. They couldn't grow into those who would inherit the promise.

Another reason one whole generation passed away before they could settle into the Promised Land was idolatry. Idolatry was a normal practice in Egypt and the Israelites did not know any better than to worship idols. Once the Israelites were out of Egypt, it took another forty years to get the Egyptian influence out of the hearts of the Israelite people. On our transition from our place of comfort to God's place of new inheritance there will be some old mentalities and ways of thinking God will need to change, and some idols we will need to tear down.

We must decide in these times if we can embrace the pain of growth here and go with the process, or like the children of Israel we can miss the inheritance because of an unwillingness to push through the process. The Lord commanded the Israelites in their freedom not to make or worship idols (not to return to their old ways), and at first, they agreed and promised not to, but went back on their word and disobeyed God (Exodus 20:4 & 34:17; Leviticus 17:7; 19:4; 26:1; Deuteronomy 27:15). Everything that could possibly be needed was set up and planned out by God for the people to enter into and enjoy their promised land. But a whole generation lost out on entering into the victory because they refused to grow amid the process.

Do not miss out on what God has positioned you up for because of a refusal to change and an unwillingness to grow. Will your growth be uncomfortable- yes! And the minute it stops being uncomfortable it's no longer growing. But remember the goal- remember the high call.

Remember that the One who sent you is still with you. That the promise is secured in Christ Jesus and therefore my obedience is all God needs to enter me into it. Will your growth have pains attached and stir up fears that you can’t handle what you’ve been given? 100% but the Word of God doesn't tell us that we won't get more than we can handle, I believe strongly to the contrary the Word simply states that

He will not give you more than He can cause you to handle.

If God has you in it He will take you through it. But don't do yourself a disservice by exiting the lane because you have mismarked your pain as suffering. Push forward towards the mark of the high call. My friend you are simply growing.

Let's pray together- God give me the endurance to put up with the pains of growth. Let me recognize your grace in each moment of push that I face. Through your Spirit let me hear the encouragement of You my Coach, cheering me forward, walking beside me. I thank you for the shaping that takes place in my growth. Today I choose to push through the pain so I might obtain growth.

Amen.

NOTES

Chapter 3

A Champion Understands That The People Surrounding Them Are Key To Their Success

Proverbs 13:20 KJV He that walketh with wise men shall be wise: But a companion of fools shall be destroyed.

Every champion beyond their coach has also surrounded themselves with an entourage of people who they truly believe are invested in their success and those people who they believe are wanting to be invested in them. Aside from your relationship with God, the relationships you build around you with other people are a key element to your success or your failure when speaking about the terms of purpose and destiny. As the line goes, if you hang out with eagles you will learn how to soar. But you can't soar like an eagle if you hang out with penguins. We need to select the right team of people around us when considering our futures. Learn to be those skilled at building a fence around yourself of people who are invested in us, and in our success, this is pivotal in holding you through inevitable moments of defeat or intimidation that will come your way.

I would go as far as to say that who you have surrounded yourself with will either push you towards or pull you away from the race God has purposed you to run. Every single relationship in our lives carries influence, don't be fooled to believe otherwise. And with this reality in mind, you need to determine whether those influences are positive or negative toward your relationship with God and the pursuit of your purpose. It is simply naive to think that those closest to you are not impacting your future. 1 Corinthians 15:33 tells us not to be deceived, bad company corrupts good morals.

Who you surround yourself with is just as important as your commitment and your self-discipline in life towards God. And because of this, bad companionship has just as much potential to derail us as a child of God as isolation does. And understanding that both these things are weapons of the enemy will help keep you on track for your kingdom purpose. Think about it in scripture no one was alone, and no one who was anyone was in foolish company, Elisha had Elijah, David had Johnathan, and Paul had Barnabas. No great hero of the bible went at it all by themselves, they all had someone attached to their life that was directly connected to their purpose, someone who was invested in their call and invested in them, and someone they in turn invested back into. This is the beauty of the Kingdom, we get to be championed by people, and in turn we get to champion others, there is no competition, there is no jealousy or bitterness, and there is only one after all who receives glory from our good works, and that is God.

I long, and pray, for a culture of the kingdom to return that truly reflects this one, as we read of in Acts- an all-for-one and one for all attitude, and one that lets go of the need to have more and be more than others. Where we as churches will promote and champion each other's events and efforts, where I can celebrate the big church around the corner and not envy it while championing the new plant down the road and not feel threatened by its presence. Man I long for the day the global church gets the revelation that we are but One Kingdom, with One King, seeking only His glory and the advancement of the one true gospel.

No one in scripture knows how detrimental the principle of good company is more than Samson, who is introduced to us in Judges 13. Samson was to be set apart by God from birth as a Nazirite, which meant as a mark of his calling, he was not supposed to touch a dead body, drink alcohol, or cut his hair. This was supposed to signify him as being set apart by God for a specific task, namely driving the Philistine oppressors out of Israel.

Early on in life, he violated the first two parts of his vow by eating honey out of a dead lion's carcass and holding a drunken feast for his wedding. But for thirty-something years of his life, his hair remained uncut. There was still some shred of physical symbol left in his life that he was set apart. Even this makes me think how sometimes we don't leave God much to work with, but a shred, and let me tell you, my God can do a lot with even a shred, so don't disqualify yourself because of your past mistakes.

Maybe you have left a lot to be desired in your standard of living before God, but today you can choose to consecrate yourself again unto your Master. Redemption after all is one of His greatest works and gifts to us. You are not unredeemable. Now Samson, as someone set apart by God for the task of driving out an enemy, was gifted with enough strength to fight as a one-man army. The idea probably was that he would encourage the Israelites that God was on their side through his great feats of strength and courage. So here he is, set apart, blessed, called by God. Everything in his life set on a trajectory of success, he was going to be the champion of champions, and he would deliver his people from the rule of the Philistines, this plan was clear from his conception. He knows this, his family knows this. And now we get back to him in the scriptures as he is choosing his wife, one of the most important relationships he will have in his life. And where does this mighty man, called of God look for his wife? Well, he chooses her right out of the camp of the enemy. Judges 16:4-5 And it came to pass afterward, that he loved a woman in the valley of Sorek, whose name was Delilah. And the lords of the Philistines came up unto her, and said unto her, entice him, and see wherein his great strength lieth, and by what means we may prevail against him, that we may bind him to afflict him: and we will give thee every one of us eleven hundred pieces of silver. Samson was so consumed with what pleased his eyes that he was ready to choose a mate straight out of the enemy's camp. To select a wife from those he was called to defeat. Begs to question of how much thought we put into the relationships we place in our lives, beyond how someone makes us feel about ourselves. They are so funny, they are so pretty, they are so popular, they are lonely just like me. Has this become our benchmark for our entourage? Do we seek out those who simply fill our emotional needs? What are the non-negotiables someone must possess to be added to our life in relationship? If you don't know the answer to this I suggest making a list and evaluating your circle from this viewpoint before you move on.

When was the last time you looked at those closest to you and asked yourself- do they champion my success? Do they promote my relationship with God? Are they there for me when it counts? When I mess up are they making excuses for me or are they elevating me to do better? Which camp are you choosing for your team today? Because some people who appear attractive to your social circle do not belong in your community. Some of our inner circle have been chosen by the standards of our low self-esteem. But let me tell you today Champions choose people who will elevate them and people who are aligned with their goals and their purpose.

Champions have people around them who aren't invested in them, for sure, but they don't choose to invest in those relationships to the same level they do, those who are. We can for sure hold acquaintance with some who we cannot afford to allow in our close community. Champions remember that they become like those they spend the most time with. If you would only choose to spend most of your time with people living to their full potential in God then guess what? You will too! If you spend most of your time with people hurt and hung up on God, given up on church and purpose then guess what? You will be too! It will be no surprise to those looking in when you follow the same steps as those you hang around. Someone once said show me your friends and I will show you your future, and how true a statement that is.

So Samson bags himself a Philistine woman named Delilah, a woman tasked to unravel his purpose, focused on derailing his purpose. And we know the story, she begs her husband to disclose the secret of his great strength numerous times. And surely Samson here must have known that Delilah was a poor influence on him, it was clear that she was trying to take from him the very thing God placed in him. How can we be so sure he knew all along that she wasn't right for him? Well, he lied to her. Each time she would ask him to share the source of his strength he would make something up. To have lied to her tells me he must have known her intentions were poor towards him from the start.

But because of how she makes him feel, because of his arrogance in himself, how he reckons he is all good and can withstand the temptation to fall. He believes he can be in this relationship and not compromise, he can have the union with the enemy's camp and not be influenced. He can remain on course for success, to be a champion even with this unequal partnership. And he must feel pretty good about himself, being led towards trouble but not getting caught, never actually compromising on who he was, he believes he is winning at this, that relationships aren't really that influential or important. Who I have around me is not that big of a deal. You're probably reading this now and forgetting it Samson we are talking about because this was or still is many of our attitudes over our lives, we longed so much for how a person made us feel that we convinced ourselves although they were not from our camp they would not do us harm.

But let me be real with you, it will come to a point in all unhealthy, unequal, unbalanced relationships that you will be called to compromise, and as strong as you think you are when pressed long enough in the wrong environment and by the wrong people you will give in to that compromise. For Samson that day came to him. Delilah pressed him with her words and urged him that if he loved her he would stop lying to her, and so the mighty Samson gives in and discloses the source of his strength, the gift of his purpose. Foolishly trusting that Delilah would preserve this secret. And yet what did she do with that? We would hope she would have learned to love him so much that she would protect his future, but no scripture tells us that immediately she gave his secret to the enemy. We must be so careful who holds our hearts. God revealed to me several years ago as a church planter that not everyone who comes to your house with a hammer is there to help you build. Don't be so trusting of superficial appearances and intentions, many motives run much deeper. Many will want to tear down the purpose of God over you. Be discerning and have wisdom concerning those you add to your life in relationship.

You can be so oblivious to the negative influence of relationships in your life that it's like they are stealing from you in your sleep. You don't see it coming until bam, they've stripped you of the champion you were set to become. Just like Delilah shaved seven locks from the head of Samson while he slept, removing him from his strength. When Samson's hair was cut, he removed the last physical vestige of his devotion to God. He rejected the symbol of God's calling, and so he rejected God's calling itself. At that point, then, God removed the strength he'd given him to carry out this purpose. Maybe you find yourself right here in the story of Samson. At a point in your life where you made choices that removed you from your devotion to

God, removed you from the call of God on you, and because of that have lost the gift or anointing that was once upon your life to live out this great call, and you're wondering if you've gone too far if God has overlooked you and moved on to someone else for this calling.

One of my favorite verses in this story is Judges 16:22 KJV- Howbeit the hair of his head began to grow again after he was shaven. Man, I love the grace of God. Think about this! After the compromise, after the mess up, after the deliberate decision to abandon the call of God, the strength he loses, the call abandoned for selfish desires, hair (strength) begins to grow back again. What a picture of the relentlessness of God concerning us. Yes, you may have messed up, you may have abandoned the call, you may have compromised. But just as the hair of his head began to grow again, as you return to God with a repentant heart, God will unknowingly to you, begin to draw you back and realign the purpose over you, to reset you and re-strengthen you.
And the story of Samson has a powerful ending. Scripture tells us that the dead which he killed at his death were more than those which he killed during his life. I love that, what God did through a redeemed Samson after he refocused, repented, and got back on track was more than he had accomplished before his mess-up. Hallelujah, Amen,

there is still hope for us all. Now we must ask, did he do everything God had destined for him? No. He only lived to complete a portion of this because of the time wasted with wrong people leading to compromise but he was still redeemable, he still had value, and God would still work with him and work through him.

My question to you now is, do you want to achieve all God has purposed over you? Then do not waste time with people who call you off track to compromise. Choose people who will champion you, challenge you for the better, and push you toward all God has called you to be. Champions understand that the people surrounding them are key to their success, do you? If so, now is the time to evaluate the relationships in your life and invest in the ones that are life-giving to the race that is set before you. And if you've already lost time with Delilah's remember you are not beyond the point of redemption and repurposing!

Let's pray-*Father God, help me to evaluate the relationships in my life. Give me discernment to fish out those relationships that are costing me my destiny and give me the wisdom to move from these places. Send the right people my way Lord, and help me befriend those who will champion my relationship with You. Spirit of God help me and shape me to also be a friend who will champion others around me, without envy, jealousy, or bitterness.*

NOTES

Chapter 4

A Champion Learns From Their Losses.

2 Corinthians 4:8-9 KJV We are troubled on every side, yet not distressed; we are perplexed but not in despair; persecuted, but not forsaken; cast down, but not destroyed.

Losing. Not a word you want to hear in a book about winning right, but the harsh truth is that losing is a natural part of life and development that we must come to terms with in order to advance effectively. As much as we prepare ourselves in this life we will simply not win at everything, every time. Some of our attempts at greatness will even end in failings, a glorious embarrassment of serious effort, and a great fat lack of results. But be comforted that all great champions have also experienced great losses. At the opening of this book, I told you that I loved track and field and have seen many champions grace the world stages from Carl Lewis to Linford Christie to Maurice Greene. All were named the fastest man in the world at one point in their career. More recently we had Usain Bolt who is still to this day renowned as the fastest human on the planet, he is well known for so many great victories as he dominated the world stage in track and field, decorated with every gold medal imaginable, eight-time Olympic gold medal winner and the only runner to ever win Olympic titles at the 100m and 200m three consecutive Olympics in a row. Simply put a beast in his field. But accompanied by all of his amazing wins he has also experienced losses on those same tracks. In 2007 Bolt lost in the World Championships 200m sprint to Tyson Gay. In 2010 he also lost the 100m Diamond League Stop in Stockholm to Tyson Gay. In 2012 he lost the 100m and 200m Jamaican Olympic Trials to Yohan Blake.

He had his fair share of losing.

But we don't remember him for any of his losses, do we? We don't choose to discount his achievements because of the handful of times he lost, he is no less a champion in my eyes or his field because he did not allow the losses he experienced to be the end of his story or the definitive mantle of his career. He didn't bow out under defeat and decide he wasn't capable of great victory, he never convinced himself that because he wasn't the best at that moment that he had no place in that field. No, instead he went and trained and learned from his loss and made sure that what went wrong in that race didn't happen in the next. I am sure he studied the tapes of his races to see where he missed that fraction of a second that cost him his medal. He would have focused on his improvement and not the other racers, he didn't note where did they beat him but centered on where he lost to them. Aware sure of the strategy of his competitors but focused on the growth of his own race.

Do you think that your worst moment in life is the point you should choose to quit? No, it's simply the point to pause - reflect - learn - grow - get back in the lane and try again, and if necessary repeat and repeat until you find success in what you are doing.

Too many people quit on the brink of victory because of an encounter with defeat. Defeat will educate you in the things that no win ever will. It will teach you that you are not indestructible, that you are not perfect, and that you don't have it all.

These are vital lessons to learn in humility as we live our lives before Christ.

But with all of that said I want you to understand that your God has not set you up to be a failure. Romans 8:37 tells us that in all these things we are more than conquerors through Him who loved us. But just because victory is secured for you in Jesus does not mean you won't experience moments of missing it and occasions of coming up short in your efforts. Even with training, dedication, commitment, and the right people around you, there will be times when the hurdle isn't cleared the first time around. There won't always be a clear reason why it didn't happen, but each moment of low in your purpose is an opportunity to pick yourself back up and go again with God.

There is a movie franchise that I hate to love, a guilty pleasure some might say. We all know of it, I'm sure there isn't a person on the planet who hasn't come across the Rocky franchise. And I hate the predictability of it, to be honest, we know how every movie will work out, he will pick a fight with a formidable opponent, he will lose to the said opponent in an almost embarrassing way, he will go lick his wounds, get back to the gym, work hard, come back and win second time round with his wife anxiously looking on from the stands. But man I love to hate them, nobody in Hollywood's history knows what it is like to lose the first time around better than Rocky Balboa, in fact, he's famous for his comebacks out of the jaws of defeat. There were seriously way too many sequels for this movie all holding the exact same structure and theme but somehow they were all big successes at the box office raking in 1.7 billion USD, making it one of the highest-grossing media franchises ever, and we as the audience resonate with each and every one, why?

Because it reflects the story we long for our life to tell, it echoes who we want to be deep down. We all identify with the first attempt Rocky, we try really hard, prepare for, train in and work towards something, and then life beats us down when we get in the ring. We all have felt the bitter sting of defeat and have spent copious amounts of time licking our wounds swearing we would never get back in the fight. The second-act Rocky, well at least for most of us, is who we wish we could learn to be the one who causes ourselves to get back up again, who learns from the loss, who grows in our weaknesses, and who takes on and beats the opposition the second time around, the one who clears the hurdle, who moves the mountain. But truthfully most of us leave the second-act Rocky to the Hollywood stories, while for us, once we lose we all too often bow out of the race and change lanes.

But can I tell you today that if that is you then God is calling you back to the arena, to reflect on what took you out the first time, maybe you were trying to achieve a God-given assignment in your human strength? Maybe you were running towards a battle you hadn't even dedicated yourself to properly preparing for. Maybe you did everything seemingly right but still got beaten by the enemy. Regardless of why you lost know this for certain- God did not lead you that far to destroy you or to fail you. This is the time to go at it again.

I pray that from today in your life you will take on bigger challenges, bigger opposition, and bigger tasks and you will free yourself from the pressure of first-time success. Become the master over things in your life that once crippled you. I vividly remember racing in an athletic community games qualifier when I was about 10/11 years old, competing in a race with kids 12/13 and I signed up for every event I could fit in to better my chance at some success. And in all the events I took part in I distinctly remember competing in the 100m hurdles, the rush of winning my heat and making it clean into the final. I couldn't believe it, to be honest, the hurdles weren't one of the disciplines that I trained in. I was thrilled with myself to get past the heats but I can clearly remember being extremely intimidated by the lineup in the finals specifically because one of the other competitors was from the same club as me, two years older than me, and always historically faster than me. Only first place in this race would move forward to the All-Ireland Finals, so the pressure was on. We lined up, the starter set us off and I couldn’t believe it- I was winning, I got out quickly and I found a great rhythm in my stride, I was actually clearing all the hurdles with ease. "I had it", I arrogantly narrated to myself down the track, I was going to represent my club in the All Ireland Hurdle final after beating our club's star athlete. That was until something dreadful happened, my pride literally became a fall, I clipped my toe on the last hurdle, only meters from the finish line and I went down, like a sad sack of potatoes, I hit the ground. The final few meters of the race lasted longer for me than the first ninety, as it seemed like everything switched to slow motion, as I watched my teammate pass me, and then another competitor, and then another and another. I can't remember but I probably finished in last place in the end. I was devastated, I shed a couple of deep yet silent tears, it was all done, I lost. I was in the lead for so long and I messed up. It didn't feel fair but it couldn't be changed, there was no do-over, and I was beaten. And at that moment I had a choice to move on or leave the day's competition a loser. I was long overdue at the long jump pit, which had been rotating athletes in my category already for a while now, so when I eventually picked myself up emotionally and made it to the side of the pit they were only allowing me one attempt. I could have decided at that moment that there was no point, that it was better not to try at all than take one jump and not succeed. After all, I had just taken a nasty fall and the other athletes had two jumps ahead of me on record, I would need one impressive jump to qualify for the All Irelands in this particular event. But instead of allowing all the reasons why I shouldn't do it dictate my actions I went to the end of the long jump track, and with everything in me I counted my strides, calculated my pace, and then ran back up the lane and I jumped. And I won, with just one jump, one attempt, I went on to the All Irelands to represent my club in both the Long Jump and the 200m in the end. I could have allowed failure or embarrassment to take me out completely but instead, I pushed on. But don't celebrate too soon, I didn't win any All-Ireland title that year, and didn't even medal, but I did get to compete. However, the truth is due to the sting of defeat in that one race I never again attempted the hurdles. I let the crush of defeat in one race, at one event, prohibit me from ever winning in something I maybe had the potential to be great in. The one win I had from this experience though was that I didn't allow defeat to completely choke me and take me out of athletics. The decision to quit competing would come later in life not because I couldn't win, I won plenty, and had racks of medals. I would later quit because all competitions would be on a Sunday and I wasn't willing to be distracted from my development and purpose in God over some natural hobby.

I can also recall my first ever Sunday morning preaching, I studied for hours and hours and it lasted a mere twenty minutes, likely because I spoke at a pace of at least a thousand words per minute. People probably did not get what I had intended them to receive from it, I didn't get showered with praise afterward, and I didn't get invitations to go speak in churches across the land, by many standards you might say I failed at delivering the preach. But imagine if I allowed the frightful experience of a first attempt to stop me from trying again. Can I just say that maturity is such an underrated quality, and although I have many areas to grow up in significantly I am so glad in life I have learned that I will not always succeed but that failing will never make me a failure. I am also so appreciative that I had people who saw beyond performance to potential and gave me another opportunity and another opportunity.

My failing simply gives me a moment to re-group, further develop, change my approach, and go again.

But just as bad as never trying again, is continuing in something without taking any learnings from the loss. Proverbs 26:11 tells us that it is like a dog returning to its vomit. Doing the same thing, again and again, is foolishness if there was no learning in between. In fact, I believe that is the definition of insanity right? To repeat the same action and anticipate a different result. If I hadn't coached myself to slow down when speaking, if I didn't do more research and study in my preparations, if I didn't begin to preach to the mirror numerous times before stepping to the pulpit, I may have very well through sheer determination have kept going in that arena, but I would have also probably continued to fail, never truly growing.

Getting back up is great, and the strength needed to try again is truly admirable, but it's simply lacking comprehension to keep trying something while avoiding the learning from the loss. Don't just run at the hurdle repeatedly, learn why you tripped on it and train yourself in that area of weakness.

You may trip several times but probably never for the same reason again.

Champions learn from their losses and by doing so experience greater victories. Failure is not the opposite of success, it's part of success. A promising junior executive with IBM involved the company in a risky venture that resulted in a ten-million-dollar loss. When brought to his boss's office to discuss, he immediately assumed the boss would request his resignation, but to this, the boss replied - are you kidding we have just spent ten million dollars educating you why would we let you go now? Morale here is that we need to take the lesson the loss is trying to teach us, don't have wasted all that energy and effort for nothing.

Remember God is still in the business of using people who have failed. The Bible doesn't paper over the failures of its heroes this is what makes it such a gripping read. Noah got drunk and exposed himself, Abraham lied twice about his wife being his sister, and Isaac did the same. Jacob deceived his father and cheated his brother. David sinned with Bathsheba and had her husband murdered. The disciples all abandoned Jesus at His crucifixion and then doubted the resurrection. Peter denied Jesus, Mark bailed out on the first missionary journey,

Moses murdered an Egyptian, and so on and so on. The Bible constantly gives us hope to know that God can use us even after we've failed. He simply needs our willingness to learn and go again.

D.L Moody said "Moses spent his first forty years thinking he was somebody. He spent his second forty years learning that he was a nobody. He spent his third forty years discovering what God can do with a nobody. "

Now if we can for a moment get back to Rocky, in the second installment we see him fight Clubber Lang, in the first fight there is so much doubt and fear in Rocky that he is defeated almost easily, the biggest change I noticed in the re-match is that Rock is no longer intimidated because he has already felt the weight of his opponent's blows before. He reviewed his fight, saw where he lost it, refocused his training, and went into the fight prepared and aware of his enemy's strategy. Clubber Lang isn't any less aggressive the second time around, he doesn't take it easy on Rocky, but what was once unknown and fearful to Rocky is now familiar territory, he goes in knowing the strength of his enemy. Some of you reading this have no idea how victorious your re-match would be if you learned from your loss and got back in the ring. The defeat has taken the fear out of the blow, so adjust what needs adjusted, train harder, and reflect on your strategy but get back in the ring with a new attitude of confidence towards your opposing enemy.

Be a champion, learn from the losses you experience in life, get back up, and allow God to help you grow in that area and go at it again. Win even if it takes a few attempts to get there, you won't be remembered for the times you tried and failed, but for the moments of victory.

Let us Pray-Father through your Holy Spirit help me to reflect on the losses I have had that have caused me to quit on things You have called me to. Give me the ability to see the areas I need to grow in. Give me the patience to work through the things I need to change. Give me the strength and courage to try again.

NOTES

Chapter 5

A Champion Doesn't Live In An Arena Of Comparison

Psalm 139:13-14 KJV For thou hast possessed my reins: Thou hast covered me in my mother's womb. I will praise thee; for I am fearfully and wonderfully made: Marvellous are thy works; And that my soul knoweth right well.

One of the hardest things to do in the pursuit of your purpose is to live in the security of who you are. I love the above scripture from the Psalms because he has gleaned just that. I am a very visual person so as I read, I see. And when I read this verse I imagine David standing in front of the mirror one morning, and upon catching a glimpse of himself, responding with- God today I praise you because you have made me so well. Ha, to have such confidence, such security. That you don't have to look further than the end of your nose to discover a reason to praise. Many of us don't have this image of ourselves in Christ, we see only the flaw, only what is yet to be completed, and we see what doesn't match up with others around us.

And comparison is so difficult to avoid and tough to defeat particularly in today's world of social media. We are confronted daily on our feed of peers and people who are pursuing a similar path to us, many of who are further on than us, have larger followings than us, and often more compliments than us. And the hard truth is that you can't really be good at anything without being compared to someone else, either as a method to inflate your ego or to bring you back down to earth. I for one absolutely struggle with this from time to time. As a singer, worship leader, preacher, pastor, writer, father, you name it, bring up any part of my life and practice and I will find you someone who does it better, bigger, and with more impact. When I compare or allow the comparison of others to sink in, I always come up short.

I often remember in my mind an interview with the late Whitney Houston from 1990 when she was asked what she thinks of her vocal rival Mariah Carey. And her response was “I don’t think of her”. Now some may say that was a dig at her competition, but I choose to believe that she was being genuine, that she could not afford to think of those who other people compared her with. Who she was and what she wanted to achieve were too important for her to get hung up on comparisons. Truth is there was room for both ladies in the world of music. And this is such a tactic of the enemy to lead us to think that purpose has to be competed for.

But be assured if God is placing you somewhere, then there is room for you, and there is room for everyone else that God sets in that area of work or ministry. You don’t have to be better than, you simply need to be no less than who God has purposed you to be.

And how freeing that message would be to us if we would only truly hear it. I am not running against anyone else. My course has one lane on it, designed uniquely for me and only me. No one competes with me for my destiny, God has cultivated a purpose for each of us. There is space for me in my race. Man, I think we should say that again but out loud - there is space for me in my race. This took me such a long time to align in my life. I am not in competition, I have already been selected by God, before I was born, before I ever did anything special or displayed any evidence of gifting, I was chosen for something of purpose to God. When we enter into competing with those around us for an opportunity then we are settling for man's opinion and approval and missing out on God's. I can remember when my youth group was going to start a youth worship band, my youth leader (and now one of my closest friends) held back on announcing who would lead the band for quite a time.

This led to speculation and expectation among all of us teens. There quickly formed opinions on who it should be, I quickly gathered a favouring view from my peers who thought I would have to be me, I already lead worship from time to time in the adult services and could sing and play keys, some others thought it would go to the pastors' daughter, she too could sing and always seemed to get these kinds of opportunities handed to her. Everyone else seemed to be ruled out of the equation, some settled they would be background singers, while others not a part at all. It mirrored something like you would see in an American school come student elections.

My supporters were arguing with the opposing supporters, each giving our youth leader their opinion on why their candidate should get the job. Until one day the youth leader was prepared to announce who had his appointment. I was just short of standing from my chair and accepting this great honor when it was announced the role would be given to the pastor's son.

We were all shocked, to this point he was the church drummer. We didn't consider him a prospect, we didn't rate him in comparison as a singer to even those who had settled themselves for the background vocals. We felt an injustice had been made. We were now considering our want to be involved in youth worship at all, I mean the audacity of it.

Before something of God had even begun, we had nearly shut it down because we were competing for something already appointed by God. And when we finally submitted to the way it was to be, we had many great times in worship together, leading in youth and adult capacities alike. See that is the clincher, we are naturally trying to compete in areas God has already set appointments. And wouldn't we truly always rather God's intention than our invention?

You can't think about comparison I suppose without being drawn to two particular men in scripture. The first of these we discover in the book of Judges where we are introduced to a man named Gideon, a young man living in a time of Midianite oppression. A people so powerful scripture tells us the Israelites made homes for themselves in the mountains and caves, in hiding. In the account we find the Angel of the Lord approach Gideon charging him with the purpose of freeing the Israelites from the hands of the Midianites, calling him a mighty warrior. A charge and encounter we would all dream of experiencing, right? A visiting angel, voicing God's specific instruction over us and marking us as mighty. That's the dream! But Gideon was so plagued with comparison he couldn't hear the beauty in the call. It must have been something he did often, so engrained in his mind and heart, because without skipping a beat he marks his family as the weakest amongst them, and himself the weakest among his family. Do you see what comparison can do? It can convince you of your weakness even when God directly calls you mighty.

I am sure Gideon always sat in the background of every discussion, challenge, and task in his family and community because he had concluded that everyone else was better than him. Have you done the same? I have. If you had placed me in a room of ten pastors as recently as a year ago I would sit back in silence, and be the one without a voice. I wouldn't have to know the calibre of the men around me even, I would simply naturally rank myself at the bottom, convinced I had no value to input, assured that I was the smallest amongst the group. I was so convinced in myself that I was the weakest in every room, I could never hear the Lord call me mighty. I never even needed anyone to tell me I was less than others, I filled that narrative in for myself for many years, plagued from childhood with comparison. But just as for Gideon whose might was in the fact that the Lord was with him, I have finally come to know that in my lane, in my purpose, I am mighty, not because I am great but because the Great One is with me. And now you cannot convince me otherwise.

And that is exactly the intent of some people around us. To convince us that we are not the ones who God would choose. Comparison isn't always self-inflicted sometimes it is cast on us from the opinions of others. Even those who may love us dearly. In 1 Samuel we see a perfect example of the injustice of comparison, as Jesse has one of his children anointed to be King of Israel. Jesse a good father excited to have raised a future King brings his children in and presents them before Samuel. All that is but one. Well after all to Jesse the one he left in the field was not comparable to his brothers for the task, he was smaller, younger, and weaker than the rest. So Jesse paraded his sons before the prophet in the order that made the most sense naturally, beginning with the biggest and strongest and working backward. When Samuel goes through all the boys and finds none are the ones who God would anoint, he asks if there are any more sons for Jesse. And Jesse realizing there was still one more didn't reveal David from the back of the line, or bring him forward from behind his back, no David was so far out of the qualifications according to his father that he had to be fetched from the fields. Man, even the people who truly love us dearly can so egregiously overlook us because they are comparing us in ways that don't matter to God. David was God's chosen, the one who He would anoint.

So honestly don't worry if others cannot identify what God has imprinted on your heart to do. Continue to be faithful to Him, serve Him right where He has asked you to and He will find you when the time is right. Even if God has to pluck you out of obscurity to set you in the place of appointment He will do so, even if no one else sees in you what God is calling out of you, it will come about.

I remember expressing to someone important to me how God had called me to pastor, and a moment I believed should have been celebrated went sour as they told me I should never be a pastor, I would be a terrible pastor, in fact, no one would like me or respond to me in that role. I was honestly the last person they thought was up for the job, and I truly believe they thought they were loving me by telling me.

Thankfully I had enough sense in me to obey the voice of God over the voice of man, but ultimately the opinion of that one man haunted me for the first five years of pastoral ministry, every time someone would leave the church I would think, huh, I guess he was right. Every time someone disagreed with my method or vision or wasn't happy with me, again 'you were warned about this'- sprung up. It actually caused me to lead for several years as a people pleaser, appointing people in roles too early because they wanted it, running myself into the ground to give a yes to everyone who asked of me. Until 2021 I burnt out. I found myself in a place hating the ministry, hating myself, frustrated with those I loved. Almost walking away from it all. I had a rough process ahead of me of identifying my issues, the main one being forgetting the one who called me in the first place.

Having to unwrap all of the opinions of others and comparisons I built around myself until all that remained was who I truly was. And let me tell you, in that moment of getting down to me, I again felt like Gideon, I am not enough. But in my weakness His strength is made perfect. I got back into proper communion with my God, and proper connection with my purpose and have lived healthy in my ministry since. Knowing that the only one I need to please is my Father. Who He has made me is enough. My truest identity is as a child of God. My workings out of that in any form of ministry or God-given task is but an additional privilege, I do not need to compete or impress because the Maker of this world has already accepted me.

The truth is that when we are focused on comparison we are distracted from really living the wonder-filled life God has laid out for us. And let's be honest none of us has that kind of time to waste, we all have busy lives, being filled with responsibilities daily, and when we aren't intentional about our destiny and our relationship with the one who crafted it, we are inadvertently flippant with our potential.

Comparison, I hope you've come to agree, is a great killer of champions. All through scripture, we see this to be true- in Cain and Abel, Esau and Jacob, and Rachel and Leah, insecurity in how God values you leads to the lie that others have access to greater favor than you when none of this is true. Stop living in the shadow of comparison and step into the light of who God has crafted you to be. Stand in front of that mirror today and realize what is looking back at you is a wonder and a reason to praise God, because you have been fearfully made, and there is no other you, nor will there ever be. And your lane is as uniquely planned as you are. So enjoy your race, no one else can run it quite like you.

Let's pray together- Father, help me see the wonder in who you have made me to be. Strip from me the need to compare with others. Allow me to celebrate others without diminishing myself. Give me the grace and strength to run in my lane. Spirit of God remove any historical damage of comparison that resides within me, set me free of the opinion of others and of self, and help me to embrace the view my Father has over me. Support me daily to grow into the image of Christ and let go of the impression of others.

NOTES

Chapter 6

Champions Always Dedicate Their Win

Hebrews 12:1-3 KJV Wherefore seeing as we also are compassed about with so great a cloud of witnesses, let us lay aside every weight, and the sin which doth so easily beset us, and let us run with patience the race that is set before us, looking unto Jesus the author and finisher of our faith; who for the joy that was set before him endured the cross, despising the shame, and is set down at the right hand of the throne of God. For consider him that enduredsuch contradiction of sinners against himself, lest ye be wearied and faint in your minds.

Every great victory speech is filled with the names of those who were on the winners' minds during the process and the stages that led them to persevere to a place of victory, included amongst those that sponsored them, and coached them, are those who the athlete or artist is now able to support because of their success and achievement.

No great champion is ever truly motivated by just the thought of personal gain, instead, they are fueled by the impact that they can make in the lives of those they love. I wonder today beyond ourselves who are we committed to winning for? Who is it we think about when the road gets too tough to continue?

For me it's an easy one- it's my son, |Josiah. As a father, I want nothing more than for my son and his generation to be able to go further in their life than I have managed to go, to get to start where I finish and carve out new ground for the Kingdom. Afterall where I am right now is the direct result of those who went and laboured before me, dedicated their lives and their energy to the furthering of the gospel, and made it so much easier for me in ministry than it would have been without their diligence, sacrifice and pressing forward. The church has come a long way in the nation of Ireland in the past 40 years and this is by no accident but through the forging of those who had us, the future, the kingdom on their minds.

I recently stood in my church building with a pastor from another local church in our city, as we talked he quickly began rejoicing in the building that we have at this short stage in our church's life. He began to tell me stories of how they started meeting in small hotel rooms, he told me of the barrier for them to be given any space at all from any business to rent for their meetings and even of the difficulty in gaining insurance for the church as they didn't fall under the tick box options for the accepted religions in our country. As he continued to unravel more tales of the faithfulness of a few which lead to breaking serious ground in my city, it gave me a renewed gratitude for how they have made it a much easier journey for young pastors like myself to come and fulfil the work God has called us to in this hour. We may now stand on fancy stages with modern systems and charity status but this was not by our doing, without the pioneering work of those before us we would be still today struggling to get a premises in which we could meet to worship.

I am forever grateful for these men and women of God who have gone before me and because of them and for those still to come I am ever more determined to continue to carve out new territory and ground for the gospel that it may continue to advance with further ease for the next generation. Even concerning the building, we are in (which we are soon enough to outgrow) man that took vision when we first viewed the property we had to duck and roll under broken shutters, use the flashlights on our phones to see anything at all as there was no working electricity.

But although we didn't see everything, we saw what could be, we saw how Drogheda could have a life-giving house in the middle of the city used by the King for the Kingdom to grow the Kingdom. We were enthusiastic at this point. But let me tell you enthusiasm, even for the things of God can fade quickly enough when the work becomes clear, trust me.

I remember the first time we saw the property in the light of day with working lighting, we were horrified, it was in way worse condition than we realized. There wasn't a wall intact in the place, half of the ceilings were missing, and the spaces as they stood were far too small to facilitate a growing church. This was going to take an investment, of money, time, and skill, most of which we didn't have a lot of. I can recall standing in what would be the main church hall during one of our workdays and turning to Brandi my wife with real fear in my eyes asking- what have we done? This space is far too small. There is way too much work to do. We have put our names on this lease. Why did we do this? And my wife reminded me quite quickly- we did this for God but also for the people of this city to have a place to find Him. This sobered my mind pretty quickly once I thought of how the kingdom would grow and how lives would benefit from our perseverance. We didn't do it for us, we never would have bothered. We did it for those who would find Jesus in this place. And that's exactly what has been happening. We now have services in 4 languages throughout the month reaching into parts of this city we never would have imagined. Kids camps English Language Tutoring and Food Banks operating out of what was a derelict building and now a house for His glory.

My wife and I often talk after every renovation or investment into the property, about how it is going to be such a blessing for the next church that needs a facility once we have moved forward. That they will be able to walk in and get to work without having to complete all the tedious tasks we needed to do and advance without spending the money we needed to spend to develop the property, it will be a turnkey property for the next growth in the move of God in our city. Sometimes some people see our development works as wasted energy and wasted finance because it is not our building but simply one we are leasing, we don't though, we never have, we see it all as an investment into the kingdom. We look at the hundreds of hours put in by us and teams of volunteers and contractors, the tens of thousands of euros spent to get our unit to the condition it is in now and we count it all as time and capital invested into the future of the kingdom, we have always been more concerned about a legacy being left than a legend being made from our own lives.

And as people of God, we need to be in the business of creating a legacy not just victory through our purpose. Future not fame needs to be our goal. To have won but not have left something for the next generation of the church to leverage off isn't much of a victory for the kingdom at all. So for that reason, we must always have others at the base of our dedication. Jesus is the foundation, others the base. Those who have made the way for us and those who need a way made for them. There have been times over the years when my wife is preparing dinner that she needs to step out of the kitchen for one reason or another and she will ask me to watch the pot. An immediate fear is struck in me every time this happens, can anyone relate? After all, I know the work she has put in up to this stage, she does not take her cooking lightly, she works hard at each meal, sometimes spending hours slicing and dicing to prepare food that our family will enjoy. Before the fork ever hits my mouth she will ask- does it taste ok? she cares that much.

And I know passing it over to me could have disastrous consequences. Likely I will get caught up on Instagram or the likes of it and forget to continue the great work she has started, "just watch it" she would say, "nothing could go wrong" she would tell me. But that's not really true now is it, I can't just sit and watch the pot and expect the meal to make itself, a lot could go wrong with the progress of the dish if I just observe. And brothers and sisters we certainly cannot just sit and watch the movement of God go by, we can't just read our Bibles and observe all the work of the men and women of God to further the gospel while we scroll through Instagram unbothered about our participation, we can't just watch the pot, we can't even afford to simply half-heartedly stir the pot. The truth is if we don't work diligently at it and contribute when it's our time that what is in the pot will eventually burn, and the taste that was intended for others to experience will be lost. And the memories and recipes we will pass onto our children from our poorly cooked food will be distorted from what was originally intended to be distributed by God.

How something so sweetly developed by the heart of God like the Church can become a bitter taste in the mouths of today's generation because of how we have altered the recipe. A dish where some of the main ingredients were once generosity and care is now confused with greed and hypocrisy. And we wonder how that happened. Could it be the result of too many years with too many people watching the pot while too few were participating in the effort?

Jesus certainly never endured the cross and overcame sin and death for His own sake, but all the time on His mind was us, the humanity He knew could be transformed by His victory. And for the world to recognize He was the true messiah some went before Him declaring the way and giving a prophecy of the one to come. Every generation working and looking forward to the next.

Legacy not Legendary is the essence of the people of God.

Romans 5:8 tells us that while we were, yet sinners Christ died for us. We were His motivation to endure the torture that was the cross, we were His reason to persevere the persecution and rejection He would face. And all while we didn't merit it. John 13:34 gives us a command to love people as Christ has loved us. Well, how did He love you? It wasn't just in words but displayed in great deeds, determination, and sacrifice. So from His command, this is how we are to carry love forward, not just in words and sentiments but in our deeds through our determination in our race and often with great sacrifice to our wants and desires. To carry people in the heart of our calling is the making of a true champion of the faith. To consider those waiting on our finish when we feel like quitting, to remember those who ran well for us to have a head start on where they began.

I am not running this race for me, I am not writing this book, pastoring my church, or serving God in any form to create for myself any legendary status, I want to leave a legacy, I won't quit or be satisfied with anything less. And so I urge you to search your heart for what motivates you like the Psalmist cry out to God and ask Him to search your heart and reveal to you if there is any selfish motive, if it is for any self-gain then re-focus is greatly needed in your life. If you are not running your race, albeit in your own lane, but if not with others at the base of your commitment you aren't paying attention.

There are too many who need you to do what God has asked you to do. Those who have faithfully finished their race are depending on you to bring the gospel to where they could not, those growing up in the faith are watching and waiting know that they need a higher base to start from than we did to complete the things God has destined them for, those who are still dead in their sin are unknowingly desperate for the light of the gospel to reach them through your purpose. If we were to win an award for our service to God and were required to give a speech, would it be filled with the names of every person who lived or would live that contributed to our success, motivated our perseverance, the ones good and bad, deserving and not, who were the reason we endured the difficulties to obtain such a victory?

I hope so. I hope that is why we are all running. I hope that is why you are doing what you are doing for God. I hope it continues through all my days to be the motivator of my heart, and that no level of human success will ever allow me to believe that I am the center of the universe.

Let us pray together- Heavenly Father give us vision beyond ourselves for the things you have called us to. Help us be more concerned with leaving a legacy and not building a legendary status. As we keep Jesus at the foundation of all we do give us those who would be the base of our perseverance. Holy Spirit allow endurance to kick in once enthusiasm has filtered out.

In Jesus Name, Amen.

NOTES

Chapter 7

Winning on Purpose

"That's Great But Now What"

James 1:23-24 For if any be a hearer of the word, and not a doer, he is like unto a man beholding his natural face in a glass: for he beholdeth himself, and goeth his way, and straightway forgetteth what manner of man he was.

I know what you're thinking now, believe me, I do. I have read many books in my life that have left me greatly inspired but often even more greatly perplexed. What am I to do with this information? How do I undo wrong habits in the pursuit of my purpose? How could I possibly motivate myself in an area of my life that is currently lacking in perseverance or discipline? In short, how do I take the words from these pages and make them part of my story?

The answer is found by no surprise in scripture! After all, everything discussed in this book is founded on biblical principles- God's wisdom is simply decorated with stories and life examples from my journey. But nothing in this book is my own intellectual property or my design. God Himself has outlined these principles in His Word. So the answer to how we live these out is also got to be found in His Word.

Zechariah 4:1-6 KJV And the angel that talked with me came again, and waked me, as a man that is wakened out of his sleep, and said unto me, what seest thou? And I said, I have looked, and behold a candlestick all of gold, with a bowl upon the top of it, and his seven lamps thereon, and seven pipes to the seven lamps, which are upon the top thereof: and two olive trees by it, one upon the right side of the bowl, and the other upon the left side thereof. So I answered and spake to the angel that talked with me, saying, What are these, my lord? Then the angel that talked with me and answered and said unto me, Knowest thou not what these be? And I said, No, my lord. Then he answered and spake unto me, saying, This is the word of the Lord unto Zerubbabel, saying, Not by might, nor by power, but by my spirit, saith the Lord of hosts.

Word and Spirit. This is it. This is how we take everything from the pages of this book and apply them to our lives. This is the source of inspiration and preparation. The well of knowledge and grace that crafts and sustains us as we run our race. We will never keep up the stamina and endurance that is necessary to win in our lanes by our own might, power, or strength. We will always come to the end of our resources if we rely solely on them. But what I have discovered is that when I have a constant stream of the scriptures into my life through daily engagement with my Bible, and when I lean into and often onto the Holy Spirit in all seasons, both the good and the bad, then I find within me the strength to remain.

Too many of us have bowed out of our great race because we have come to the end of ourselves. Never truly realizing that we are never meant to be the source of our strength. His strength has the opportunity to be made perfect in our weakness. God has never challenged you to prove yourself in your journey of life, but often in scripture, He does invite you to test Him. Why? Because He wants to be the provision for your vision, the curator of your dreams, the custodian of your future. And if we could learn that we could start to live a life that allows God to glorify Himself through us instead of one that is trying to find glory in the sight of God.

We would discover His plan and happily trade our own in exchange to live His. We would find the grace to deal with the pains that accompany our growth. We would discern our relationships with the help of the Holy Spirit and surround ourselves with those appointed and anointed to walk alongside us. Our losses would not destroy us but direct us to greater victories. We would never be caught up in the trap of comparison because we are being fed daily the truths of God's love for us, and the individuality of His design within us. And we would hold His heart in us- doing what we do for His glory and others' advancement.

I cannot emphasize enough how much true joy and fulfilment are found in the individual purposes of God. How much freedom is waiting to be experienced and enjoyed in YOUR LANE? I have run so many years of my Christian life in a competing circuit that I fabricated for myself. Thinking I had to be better than, wiser than, and more gifted than everyone around me to be significant. But then one day I got it- significance is already within me. I am not searching for it, I am working it out. Value is already upon me, I am not competing for it or earning it before my God. I am not actually in a circuit, or on a race track, I am on a road, a road designed for me, with many bends and corners that are actually protecting my faith.

Because the reality is if I saw all God had purposed for my life I would not yet have the faith to believe Him for it. My faith is crafted through every small stretch of road, every minor hurdle and challenge, and every piece of purpose I get to walk in and walk through. It is a long road, one I run on, walk on, stumble on, get back up, and continue on. It's one I alone am designed to travel but one I am never intended to travel on alone. I have God, His Word, and His Spirit on this journey. I have relationships appointed for moments and seasons to support, challenge and pray for me.

I have NEVER had this much fun in my life doing ANYTHING else other than what God has purposed for me. So I invite you to the freedom of your destiny. To the most learning, stretching, yet freeing and fun experience you could ever have! I have yet to hear someone regret at the end of their lives the things they had done with God, but I have heard many regret the things they never dared to do. People love to say Let Go and Let God, but I want to challenge you to Grab Hold and Watch God work wonders in the area of your destiny!

Let's pray one final time together: Father God, firstly I want to sincerely thank you for placing value on me and putting significance within me. Before I earned your attention you called me to great participation in Your Kingdom. Today I commit myself to Your purpose over me. I dedicate myself to Your Word and Your Spirit. Today I step onto my lane. Today I say YES. From this moment I will live like the Champion You have designed me to be. Within your grace, and firmly in my place. Amen.

NOTES

NOTES

NOTES

References

All Scripture used throughout this book is from the KJV.

Reference is made to the following:

Facing the Giants (2006) written by Alex Kendrick, The Karate Kid (1984) written by Robert Mark Kamen, The Rocky Movies (1976) written by Sylvester Stallone, Whitney Houston interview (1998), Usain Bolt, D.L Moody

All Referencing was draw from opinion and is offered simply as a mirror to the principles within the book. The statements made about each item are brief quotations embodied in critical reviews and certain other non-commercial uses permitted by copyright law.

To contact the author please email: **pastor.david@nlfc.ie**

Printed in Great Britain
by Amazon